Sock Monster and the Trees!

NARRATED BY THE SOCK MONSTER...
WRITTEN AND ILLUSTRATED BY

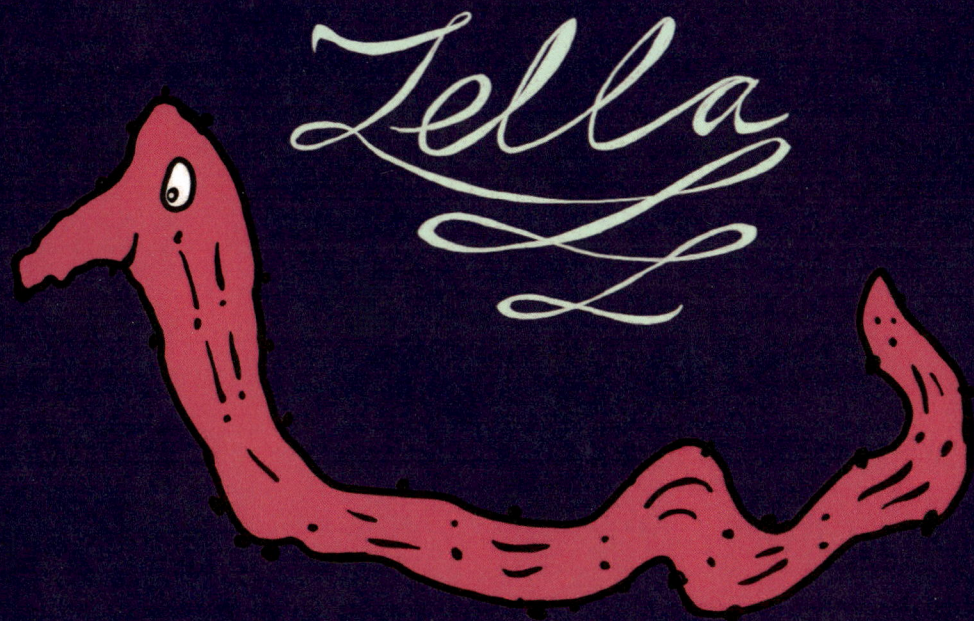

Zella

Zella Books Limited
www.zellahunter.com
This Zella Books paperback edition published 2022

1

First published in paperback by Zella Books 2022
Copyright © Zella Books Limited 2022

Katherine Studholme asserts the moral right to be
identified as the author of this work under the pen
name Zella Hunter

A catalogue record for this book is available from
the British Library

ISBN 978-0-9928865-1-6 Paperback
ISBN 978-0-9928865-2-3 Hardback
ISBN 978-0-9928865-3-0 Epub

www.kidsstoptheclock.com

TREES AND ME

'WHAT IS THIS?' ASKED THE SOCK MONSTER.

A tree!

'WHAT IS THIS?'

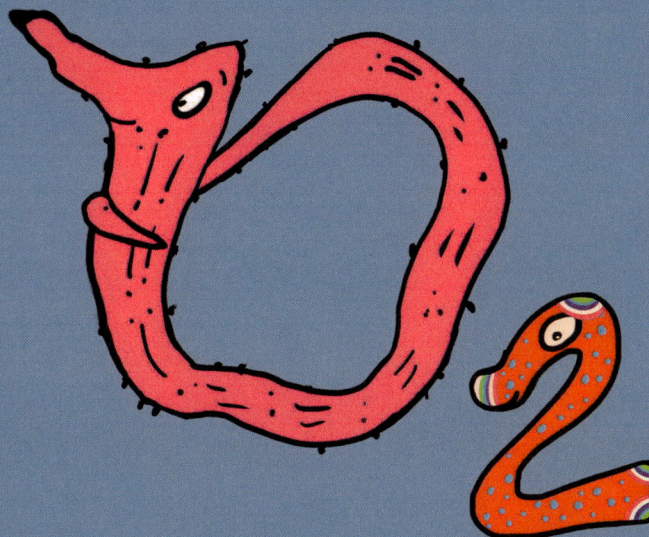

Oxygen.

'WHAT IS THIS?'

Carbon dioxide.

'WHAT DO WE BREATHE IN?'

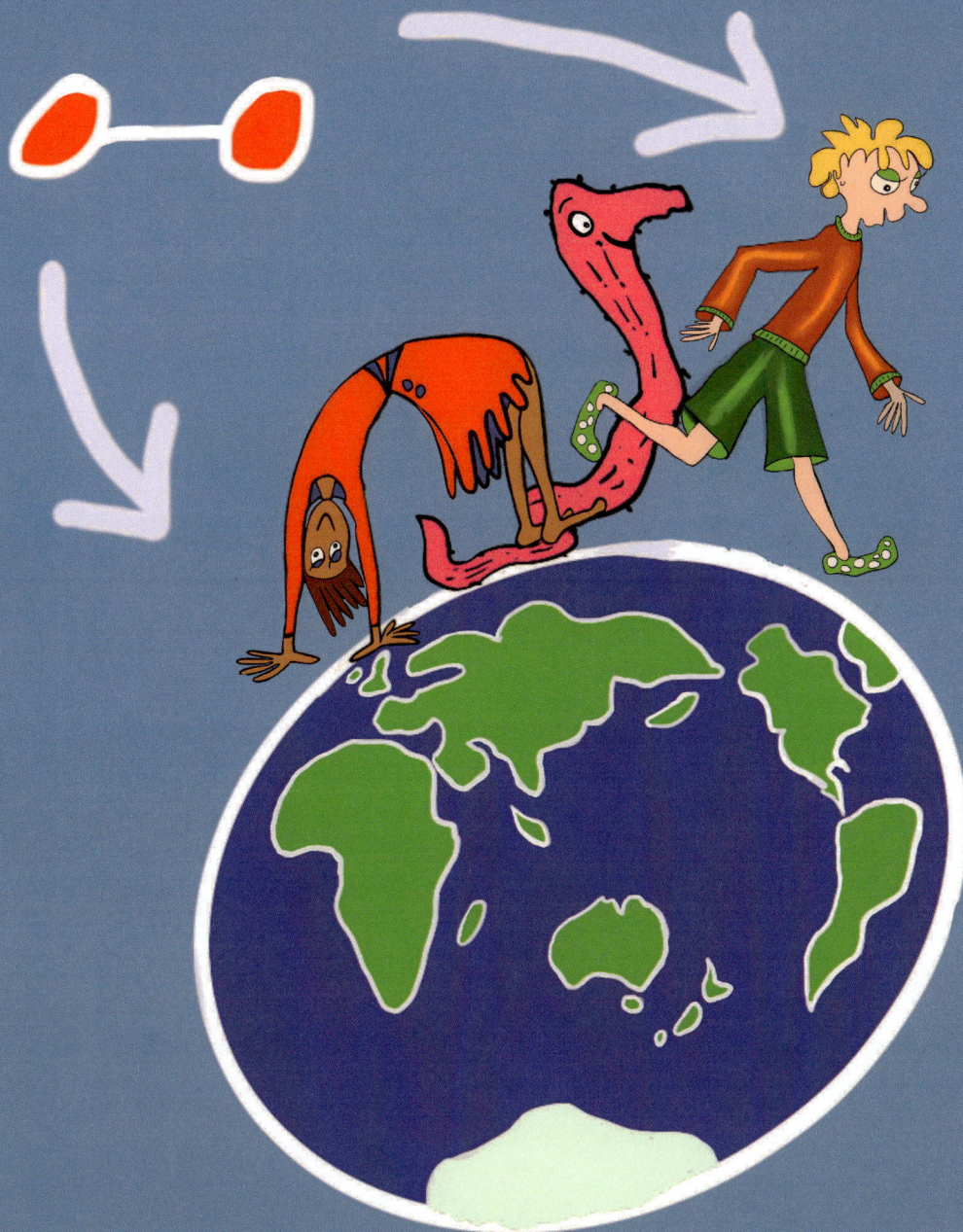

Oxygen.

'WHAT DO WE BREATHE OUT?'

Carbon dioxide.

'WHAT DO TREES BREATHE IN?'

Carbon dioxide.

'WHAT DO TREES BREATHE OUT?'

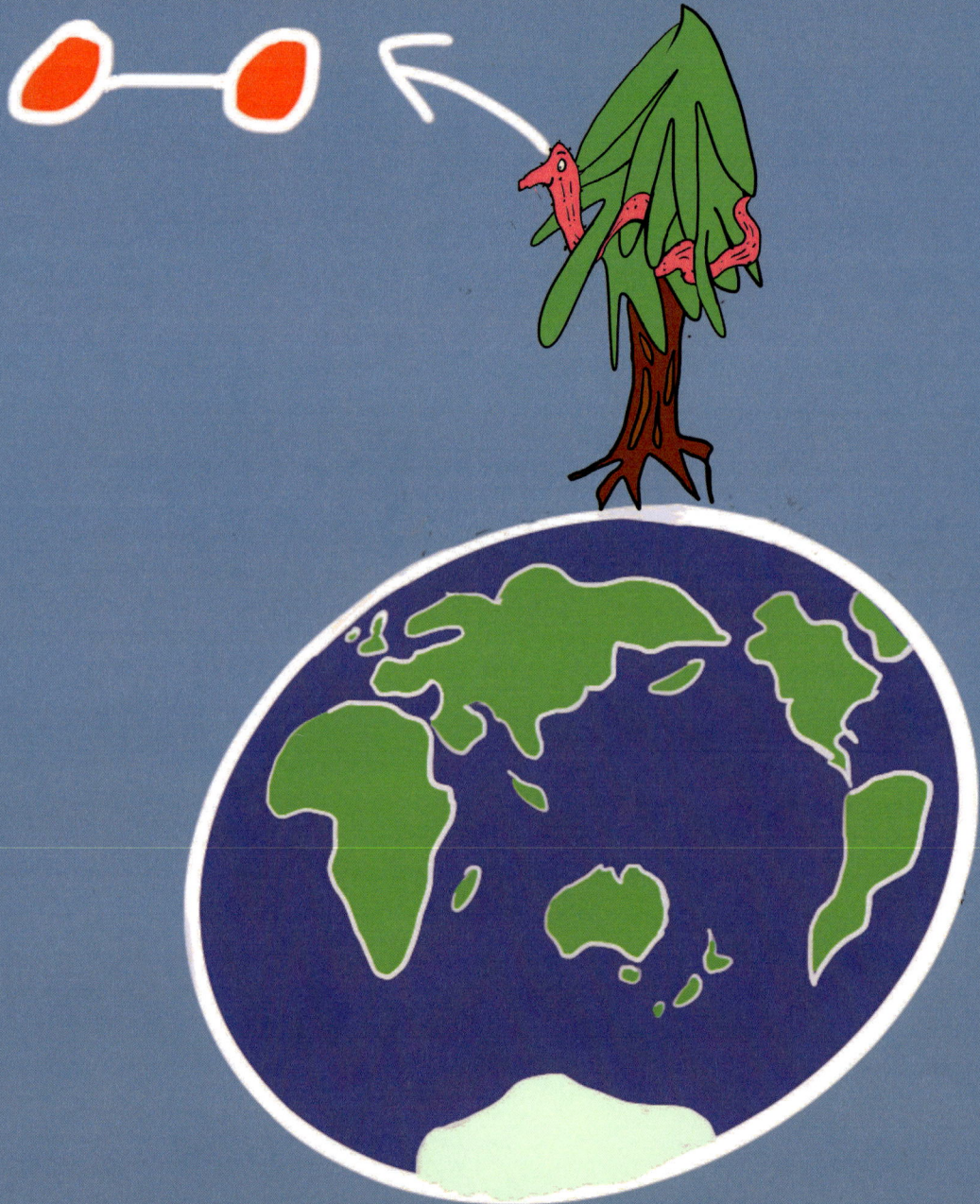

Oxygen.

'WHAT DO OCEANS ABSORB?'

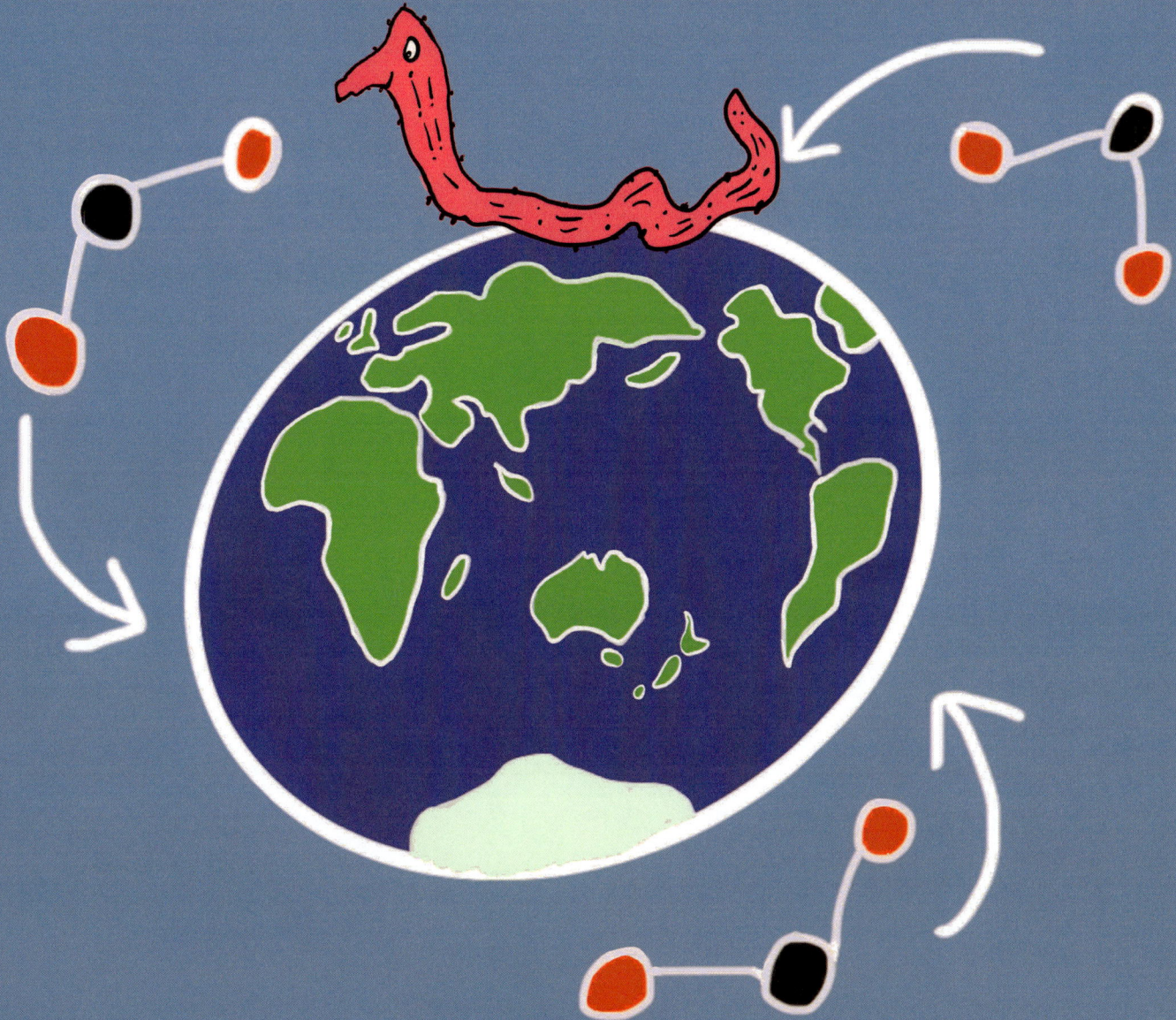

Carbon dioxide.

'WHY IS THIS SO SPECIAL?'

Oxygen and carbon dioxide help give and sustain life. Trees, oceans and humans rely on each other – this is called a symbiotic relationship.

Can YOU say that out loud?
Sym - bi - o - tic!

Oceans and trees use carbon dioxide and release oxygen.

Humans breathe in the oxygen and breathe out carbon dioxide.

'WHY DOES THIS MATTER FOR US?'

One tree could create oxygen for three people, maybe more.

Tiny plants in the sea (plankton) create at least half of the earth's oxygen.

WHAT IS HAPPENING TO OUR TREES?

'HUMANS ARE CHOPPING THEM DOWN!' SAID THE SOCK MONSTER.

15 billion trees a year. We cut down
2 trees per person each year.

'WHERE DOES PAPER COME FROM?'

A truck!

To you!

A tree!

A factory!

A shop!

'WHAT DO WE MAKE WITH TREES?'

We build houses and furniture.

We also make cardboard and packaging.

'WHY ELSE DO WE CHOP DOWN TREES?'

To clear land and then grow food, biofuel or palm oil. Palm oil is used in many products - including cake, crisps, chocolate and cleaning products.

WHEN WE CHOP DOWN TREES, WITHOUT REPLANTING TREES, IT IS CALLED DEFORESTATION.

Can YOU say 'de - fo - rest - ation?

Can YOU find some creatures who lose their rainforest home because of deforestation?

* 16 rainforest creatures on page 42

'PEOPLE ALSO BURN OUR TREES TO GET MORE LAND!' EXCLAIMED THE SOCK MONSTER.

Burning the trees hurts the air because the fire releases soot (black carbon).

We have lost large amounts of rainforest through deforestation.

WHAT IS HAPPENING TO OUR AIR?

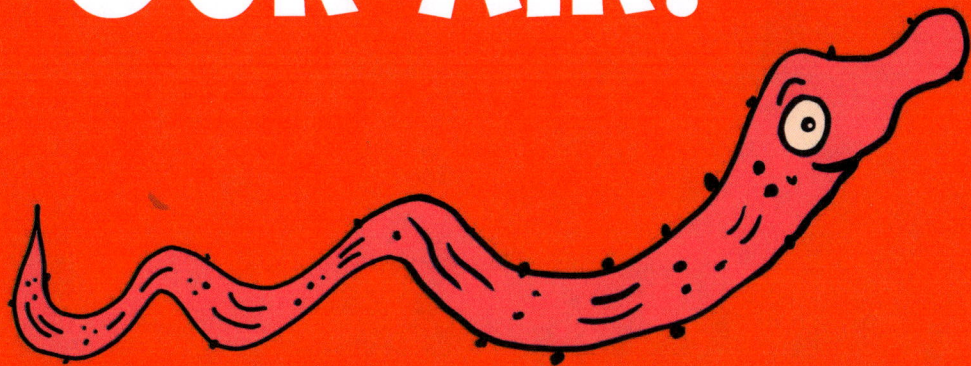

'WHAT IS HAPPENING TO OUR AIR?' ASKED THE SOCK MONSTER.

There is more carbon dioxide, and other greenhouse gases, in the air. The air becomes unbalanced.

'WHAT DO GREENHOUSE GASES DO?'

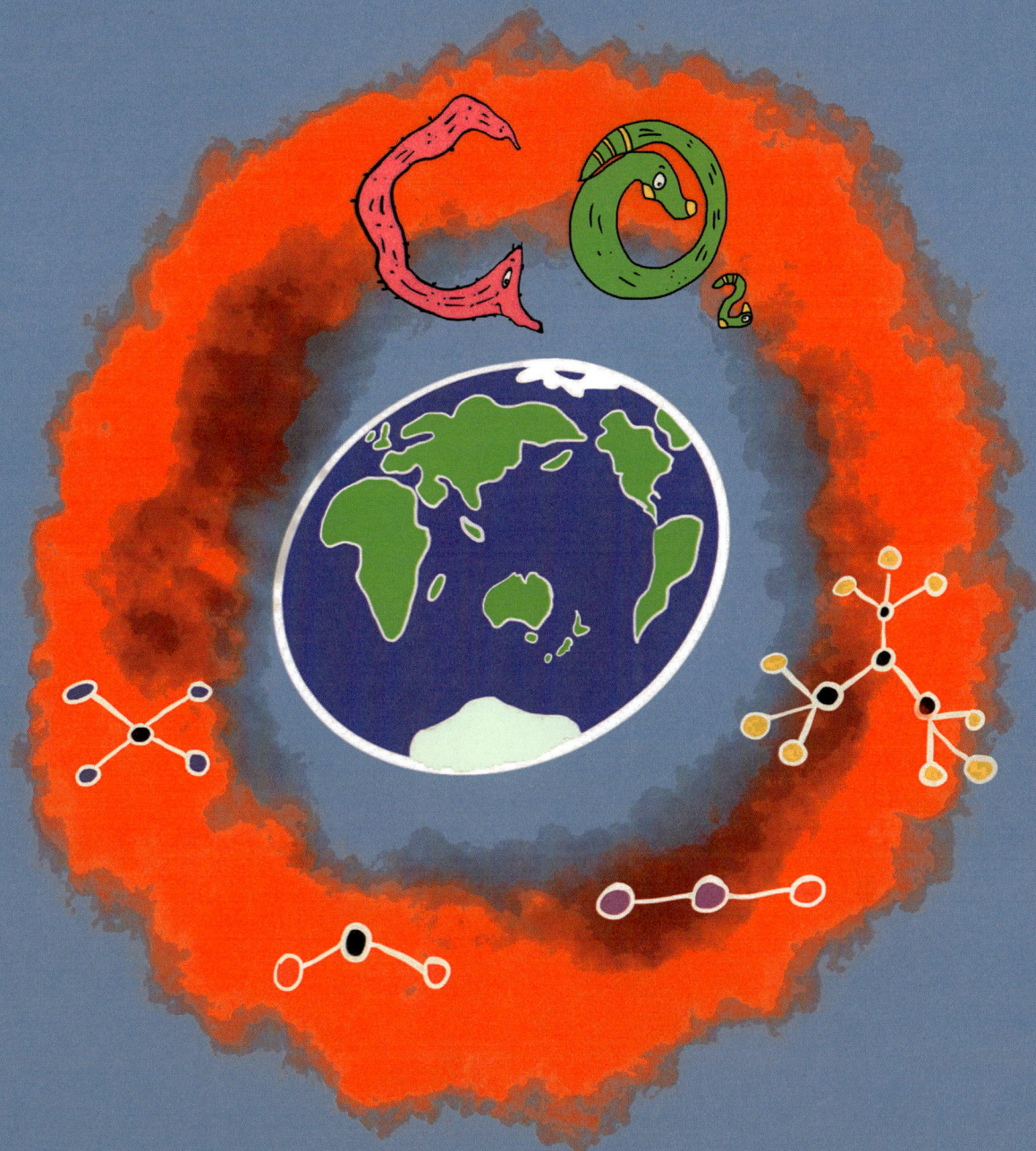

Absorb the sun's energy. The greenhouse gases create a warm blanket of air around the earth.

'WHERE HAVE THESE GASES COME FROM?'

Human activity creates these gases.

For example, we create greenhouse gases when we drive cars, fly planes, sail on cruise liners, ship with tankers, burn fossil fuel (oil, gas, coal), deforest land, make cement, build... Large amounts of methane are created by cows!

Would YOU like to change anything in this picture?

'WHAT IS HAPPENING TO OUR CLIMATE?'

Our earth is getting hotter.

'WHAT IS HAPPENING AT THE EQUATOR?'

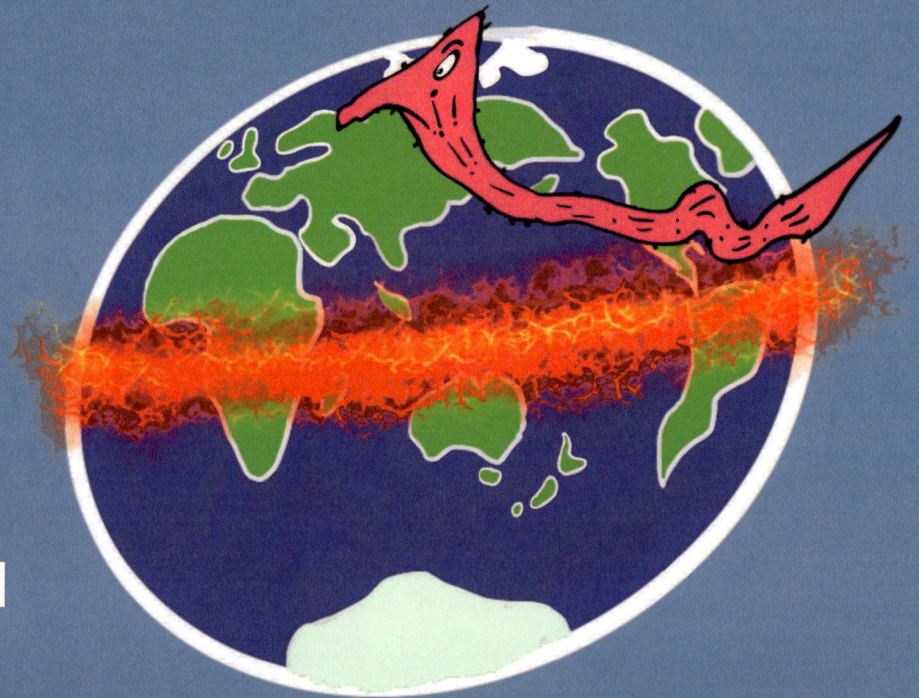

It is the hottest place on earth, and often called the tropics.

Temperatures are rising more slowly in the tropics, compared to the North and South Poles, but water in the air (humidity) makes it harder for people to cool down in a hot place like the tropics.

If the temperatures were to increase, by even 2 or 3 degrees, with more humidity, it could become hard to live near the equator.

'WHAT IS HAPPENING AT THE NORTH AND SOUTH POLES?'

The ice is melting. The ice changes to water.

The water goes into the sea. The sea levels rise. This is bad for people living near the coast.

Can YOU think of any other animals who might struggle as the ice melts?

'HOW DOES THE WATER GET INTO THE AIR?'

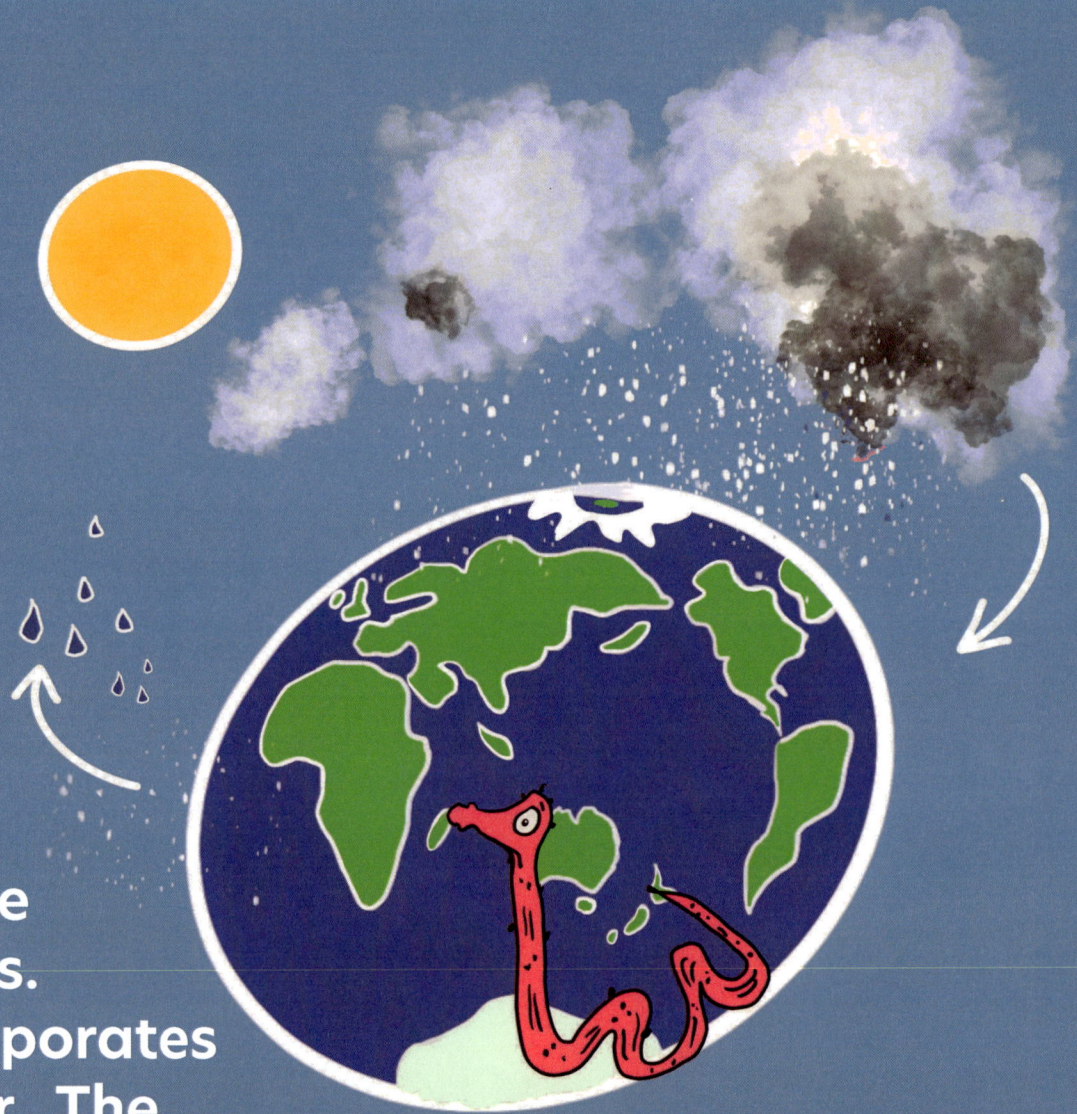

The sun shines. The sea steams. Water evaporates into the air. The droplets of water collect high in the sky as clouds.

When the earth is warmer, more water evaporates from the sea. When there is more water in the air, then there are more storms.

'WHAT IS HAPPENING TO OUR WEATHER?'

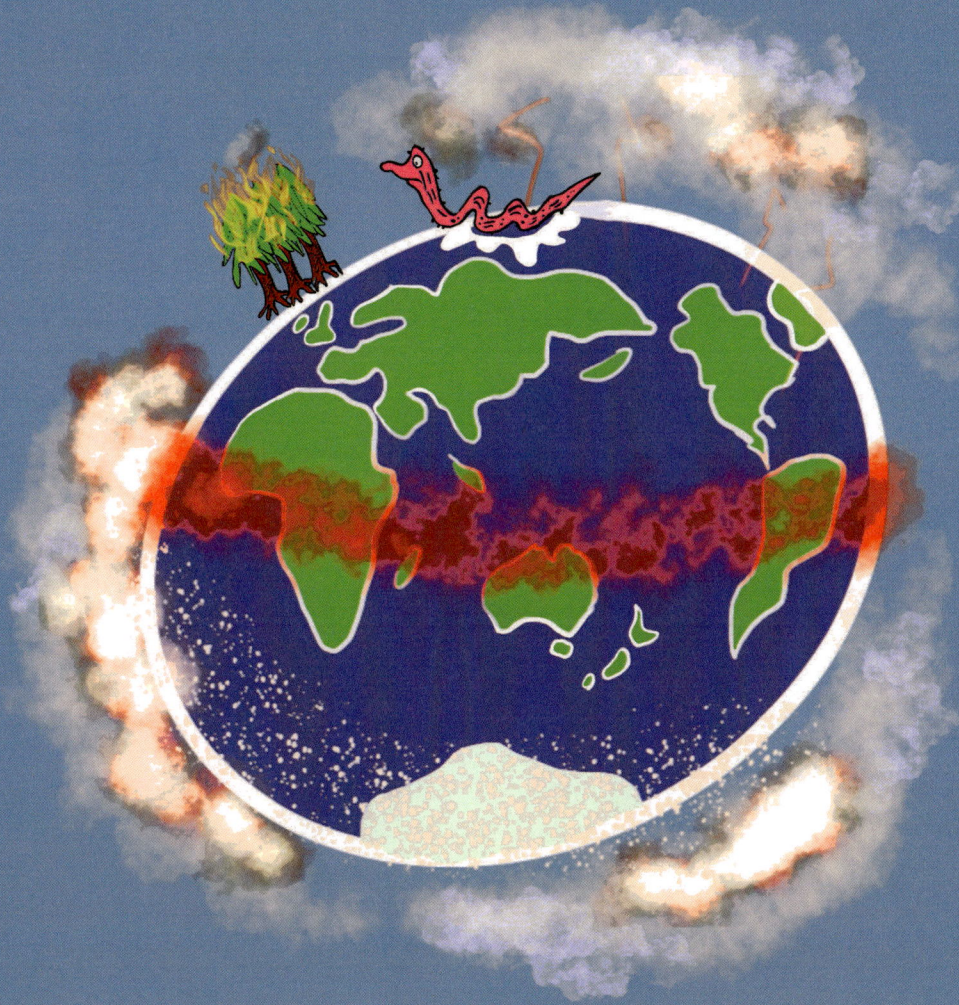

When the ice melts and our world gets warmer, the weather everywhere becomes more extreme.

Can YOU see what is happening to the weather?

There are more storms, floods, heatwaves, droughts and wildfires!

HOW CAN WE HELP THE TREES AND OUR WORLD?

'WHAT CAN WE DO TO BE KIND TO OUR EARTH?' ASKED THE SOCK MONSTER.

Plant trees

'WHAT ELSE CAN WE DO?'

Buy less. Everything we buy has a carbon footprint. A carbon footprint means that carbon dioxide or other gases are released into our air when we buy and make things.

'WHAT HAPPENS WHEN WE BUY LESS?'

When we buy less there is less cardboard being wasted.

'ARE THERE OTHER WAYS TO HELP?'

Recycle paper. Recycling is better than using virgin paper from trees.

'WHAT ELSE CAN WE DO?'

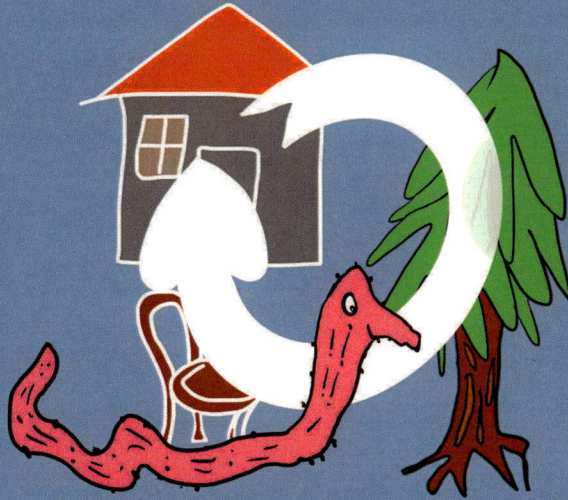

Build less. Build greener. It is better for our earth to renovate, restore and revive buildings and furniture, rather than to build using new materials.

'WHAT CAN WE DO TO HELP OUR RAINFORESTS?'

We can stop buying things with palm oil in them. We can choose food that is local and in season.

Can YOU think of some good questions to ask before you buy a product?

For example, 'what is this made of?'; and 'where does it come from?'

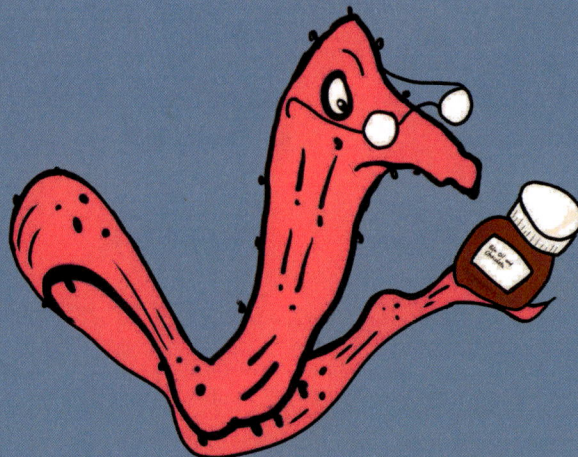

'REMEMBER, BE KIND, THINK AND MAKE BETTER CHOICES: EACH CHOICE MATTERS!' SAID THE SOCK MONSTER.

What do YOU see that you like in this picture?

Choose better! Think about trees

Be kind to EARTH

♥ ♥ ♥

www.KidsStopTheClock.com

GLOSSARY OF GASES

Oxygen - O_2

Carbon dioxide - CO_2

Nitrous oxide - N_2O

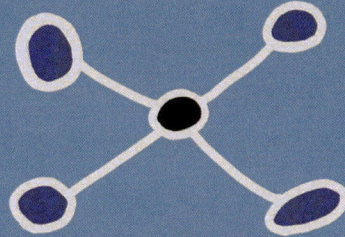

Methane - CH_4

Water - H_2O

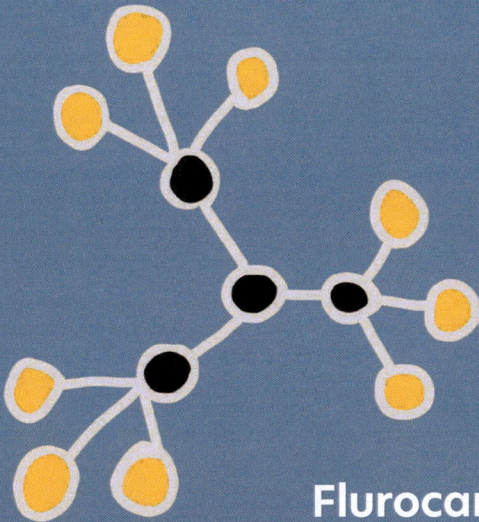

Flurocarbon - C_XF_Y

Greenhouse gases - all of the above (except oxygen, although when it forms as O_3 ozone can be a greenhouse gas depending where it is in the atmosphere). We have enough oxygen to breathe! Our world's dry atmosphere contains 78% nitrogen, 20.9% oxygen, 0.934% argon, 0.0417% carbon dioxide and 0.000187% methane. 0 to 3% is water vapour. Changes in the balance of our air impacts on climate change.

RAINFOREST CREATURES

Orangutan

Jaguar

Bat

Scarlet Macaw

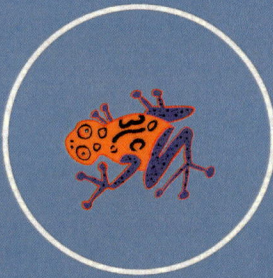

Red and Blue Poison Dart Frogs

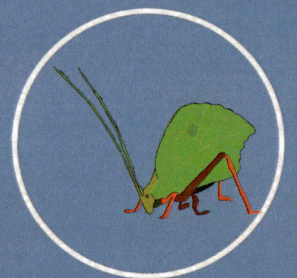
Tree Frog

Katydid

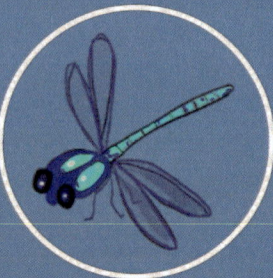
Dragonfly

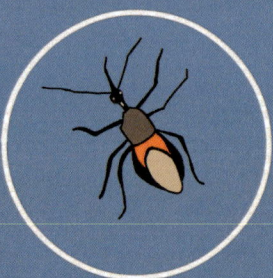
Assassin Bug

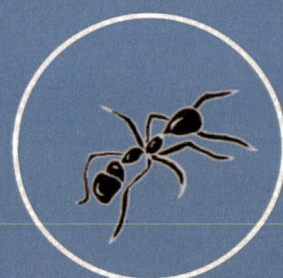
Bullet Ant

White Hag Moth

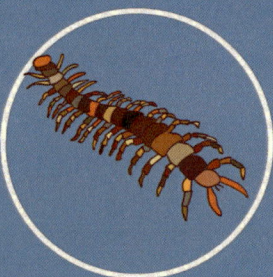
Giant Centipede

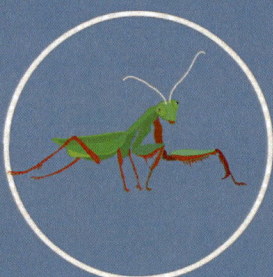
Praying Mantis

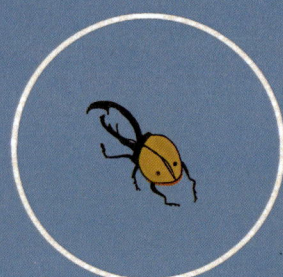
Hercules Beetle

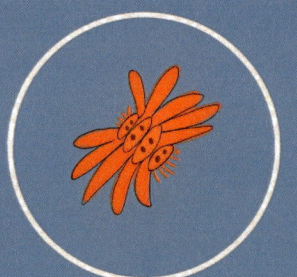
Monkey Slug Caterpillar

FIERCE BAD FACTS AND DEFINITIONS

Landfill - When we throw things away, without recycling, it goes into 'landfill'. Over 26% of landfill is paper/cardboard. As paper decomposes it releases methane. Methane is 30 times worse than carbon dioxide at warming the earth.

Photosynthesis - Photosynthesis describes how plants, algae and some bacteria (cyanobacteria) take carbon dioxide, water and sunlight and turn it into food (sugar) and oxygen.

Plankton - 'Plankton' is from the Greek for 'wanderer' or 'drifter'. Plankton are very small and found in the sea - some are plants (phytoplankton) and others are microscopic animals (zooplankton). Zooplankton eat phytoplankton. Scientists estimate that 50 to 80% of the oxygen on earth is from the ocean - and the majority of this oxygen production is from ocean plankton, seaweed and algal plankton (when they photosynthesize).

Silviculture - Silva is Latin for 'forest', and cultura is Latin for 'growing'. Silviculture is the science and art of growing and cultivating tree crops. It is important that we grow and manage trees. We need to manage trees so we keep the right balance to help us build things sustainably, to make books and to breathe! In the West, we tend to be increasing the number of trees. However, in developing countries, deforestation is more common.

Tree charities - If you want to plant a tree here are some great websites: www.treesforjane.org supporting the work of Dr Jane Goodall and www.1t.org which creates a platform to conserve, restore and grow one trillion trees by 2030.

United Nations - The United Nations (UN) is an international organization founded in 1945 to promote peace and international co-operation between countries. The UN examines evidence on how children will be exposed to climate dangers and has concluded that it will be very bad for one billion children. The report can be found here www.unicef.org. The UN has 17 global goals and goal 13 is Climate Action.

FIERCE BAD FACTS ABOUT PALM OIL

Palm oil is a very high-yielding oil compared to other vegetable oils, and it is used in many products – over 60% of products in our supermarkets use palm oil. It can be found in biofuel, cleaning products, food and other goods. Growing more palm oil crops affects wildlife and local people as the forest is cleared to put in new palm oil plantations. Orangutans, Asian elephants, tigers, gorillas and buffalo are just some of the wild animals affected by deforestation.

Palm oil has over 200 names.
Ways to spot it in your
supermarket include:

(1) the label will say it
    contains something with
    the word 'palm' in it; or
(2) the ingredients look like they
    could be used in a chemistry
    experiment.

Palm Kernel
Palm Kernel Oil
Palm Fruit Oil
Palmate
Palmitate
Palmolein
Palmitic Acid
Palm Stearine
Palmitoyl
Palmitoyl Tetrapeptide-3
Hydrated Palm Glycerides
Ethyl Palmitate

Octal Palmitate
Palmityl Alcohol
Glyceryl Stearate
Stearic Acid
Elaeis Guineensis
Oxostearamide
Sodium Laureth Sulfate
Sodium Lauryl Sulfate
Sodium Kernelate
Sodium Palm Kernelate
Sodium Lauroyl Lactylate
Sodium Lauryl Sulphate

A good source for the 200 names can be found here
www.orangutanalliance.org

WWF recommends that people look for the sustainable palm oil label 'RSPO', which stands for the 'Roundtable on Sustainable Palm Oil': www.rspo.org

For Bill Studholme, a man of the trees!

And for Sebastian, Charlotte, Matilda, Miss Lavinia
and all their friends and children everywhere!

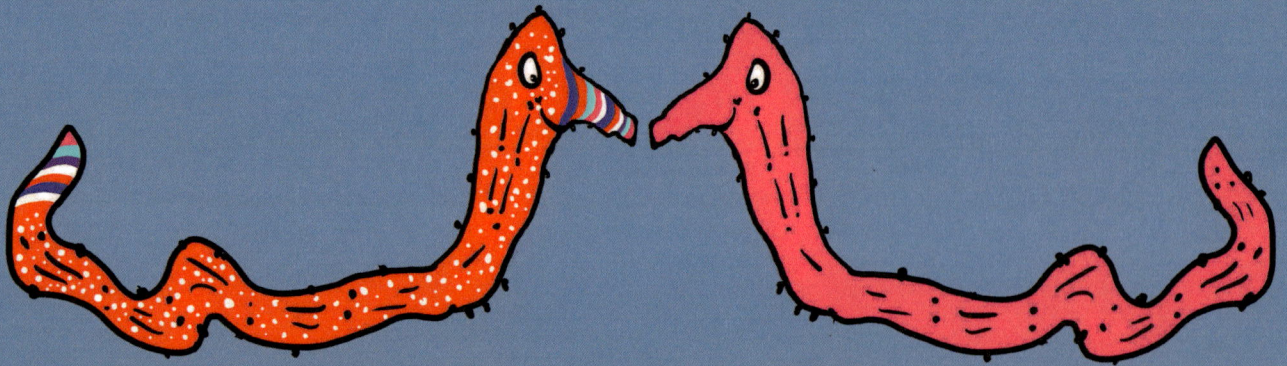

Kneelicker and the Sock Monster
are great friends!

COMING SOON
Sock Monster and the Money-Go-Round

www.ingramcontent.com/pod-product-compliance
Lightning Source LLC
Chambersburg PA
CBRC090821090426
42737CB00006B/118